HERMIONE GRANGER

HARRY POTTER STUDENT TURNED HEROINE

KENNY ABDO

Fly!
An Imprint of Abdo Zoom
abdobooks.com

abdobooks.com

Published by Abdo Zoom, a division of ABDO, P.O. Box 398166, Minneapolis, Minnesota 55439. Copyright © 2021 by Abdo Consulting Group, Inc. International copyrights reserved in all countries. No part of this book may be reproduced in any form without written permission from the publisher. Fly!™ is a trademark and logo of Abdo Zoom.

Printed in the United States of America, North Mankato, Minnesota.
102020
012021

THIS BOOK CONTAINS
RECYCLED MATERIALS

Photo Credits: Alamy, Everett Collection, Newscom, Shutterstock,
©Folger Shakespeare Library p10, p11 / CC BY-SA 4.0
Production Contributors: Kenny Abdo, Jennie Forsberg, Grace Hansen
Design Contributors: Dorothy Toth, Neil Klinepier, Laura Graphenteen

Library of Congress Control Number: 2020910910

Publisher's Cataloging-in-Publication Data

Names: Abdo, Kenny, author.
Title: Hermione Granger: Harry Potter student turned heroine / by Kenny Abdo
Other title: Harry Potter student turned heroine
Description: Minneapolis, Minnesota : Abdo Zoom, 2021 | Series: Fierce females of fiction | Includes online resources and index.
Identifiers: ISBN 9781098223120 (lib. bdg.) | ISBN 9781098223823 (ebook) | ISBN 9781098224172 (Read-to-Me ebook)
Subjects: LCSH: Granger, Hermione (Fictitious character)--Juvenile literature. | Harry Potter films--Juvenile literature. | Witches--Juvenile literature. | Wizards in literature--Juvenile literature. | Heroes--Juvenile literature. | Characters and characteristics in literature--Juvenile literature.
Classification: DDC 809.3--dc23

TABLE OF CONTENTS

HERMIONE GRANGER

Hermione Granger went from Hogwarts' resident **overachiever** to one of its most loyal protectors.

Granger was a key part of the Harry Potter **franchise's** heroic trio, which included Ron Weasley and Potter.

BACKSTORY

Author J.K. Rowling based Granger a bit on herself. She was also called a "know it all," while trying hard to succeed. Rowling was firm in having a strong female character in the series.

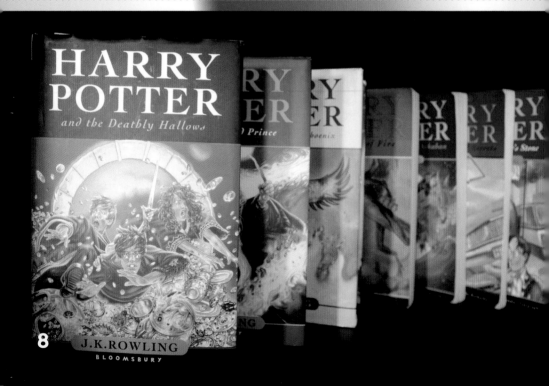

9

Rowling found the name Hermione in *A Winter's Tale* by William Shakespeare. She liked that the name was unique. But doesn't think her Hermione and Shakespeare's has much in common.

Granger first appears in *Harry Potter and the Philosopher's Stone*. She meets Harry and Ron on the Hogwarts Express. There, the series-long friendship begins.

JOURNEY

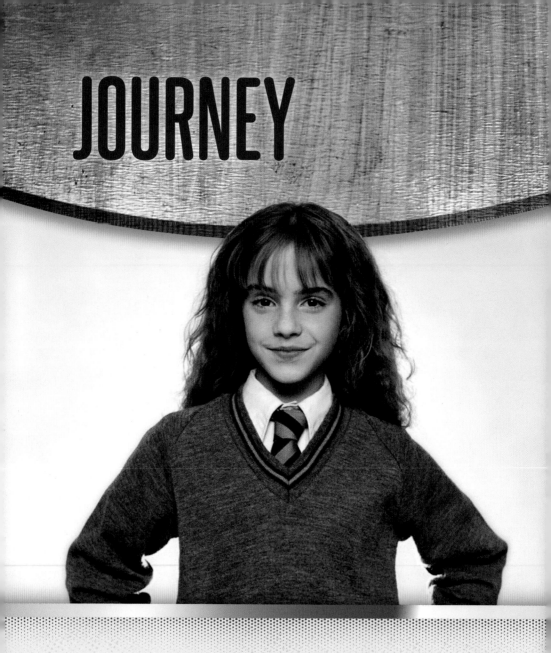

Granger was born in 1979 to **muggle** parents. By age 11, she had learned about her magical powers. Granger was then accepted into Hogwarts.

The Sorting Hat originally wanted to put Granger in Ravenclaw. It is a house known for wisdom and cleverness. However, she was ultimately sorted into Gryffindor.

Granger uses her intellect and her wand to fight. When her vine wood wand is taken by the Snatchers, Granger resorts to using Bellatrix Lestrange's wand.

Granger was a crucial fighter in the Battle of Hogwarts. She helped defeat Bellatrix and other villains to reclaim their school from Voldemort.

Granger married Ron after leaving Hogwarts. She joined the Department for the Regulation and Control of Magical Creatures. In 2019, she became the new **Minister for Magic.**

EPIC-LOGUE

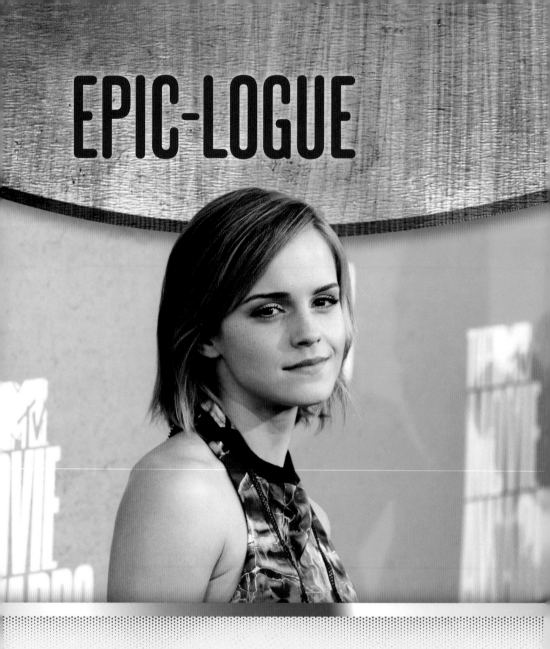

Emma Watson is the main actress to play Granger. It was her very first **role**. She auditioned nine times before landing the part at the age of nine.

Appearing in video games, novels, theme parks, and movies, Hermione Granger has cast a spell on the world.

GLOSSARY

franchise – a collection of related movies in a series.

Minister for Magic – the political leader of the wizarding community in the UK and Ireland.

muggle – a person who has no magical blood or abilities.

overachiever – a person who strives to achieve success above the standard.

role – a part an actor plays.

ONLINE RESOURCES

Booklinks
NONFICTION NETWORK
FREE! ONLINE NONFICTION RESOURCES

To learn more about
Hermione Granger, please
visit **abdobooklinks.com**
or scan this QR code.
These links are routinely
monitored and updated to
provide the most current
information available.

INDEX